The Shining Gateway

T0166051

JAMES ALLEN TITLES

The Shining Gateway

James Allen

MEDIA

Published 2019 by Gildan Media LLC
aka G&D Media
www.GandDmedia.com

Design by Meghan Day Healey of Story Horse, LLC

Library of Congress Cataloging-in-Publication Data is available upon request

ISBN: 978-1-7225-0245-4

10   9   8   7   6   5   4   3   2   1

Contents

Editor's Foreword

Students of the works of James Allen all over the world will welcome with joy another book from his able pen. In this work we find the *Prophet of Meditation* in one of his deepest and yet most lucid expositions. How wonderfully he deals with fundamental principles! Here the reader will find no vague statement of generalities, for the writer enters with tender reverence into every detail of human experience. It is as though he came back to *The Shining Gate*, and, standing there, he reviewed all the way up which his own feet have travelled, passing over no temptation that is common to man; knowing that the obstacles that barred his ascending pathway, or the clouds that at times obscured his vision, are the common experiences of all those who have set their faces towards the heights of Blessed Vision. As we read his words now, he seems to stand and beckon to us, saying, "Come on, my fellow Pilgrims; it is straight ahead to the Shining Gateway; I have blazed the track for you." In sending forth this, another posthumous volume from his pen, we have no doubt but that it will help many and many an aspiring soul up to the heights, until at last they too stand within *The Shining Gateway.*

—Lily L. Allen
Bryngoleu,
Ilfracombe, England

The Shining Gateway of Meditation

Be watchful, fearless, faithful, patient, pure:
By earnest meditation sound the depths
Profound of life, and scale the heights sublime
Of Love and Wisdom. He who does not find
The Way of Meditation cannot reach
Emancipation and enlightenment.

The unregenerate man is subject to these three things—*desire, passion, sorrow*. He lives habitually in these conditions, and neither questions nor examines them. He regards them as his life itself, and cannot conceive of any life apart from them. Today he desires, tomorrow he indulges his passions, and the third day he grieves; by these three things (which are always found together) he is impelled, and does not know why he is so impelled; the inner forces of desire and passion arise, almost automatically, within him, and he gratifies their demands *sans* question; led on blindly by his blind desires, he falls, periodically, into the ditches of remorse and sorrow. His condition is not merely unintelligible to him, it is unperceived; for so immersed is he in the desire (or self) consciousness that he cannot step outside of it, as it were, to examine it.

To such a man the idea of rising above desire and suffering into a new life where such things do not obtain seems ridiculous. He associates all life with *the pleasurable gratification of desire*, and so, by the law of reaction, he also lives in the misery of afflictions, fluctuating ceaselessly between pleasure and pain.

When reflection dawns in the mind, there arises a sense (dim and uncertain at first) of a calmer, wiser, and loftier life; and as the stages of introspection and self-analysis are reached, this sense increases in clearness and intensity, so that by the time the first three stages are fully completed, a conviction of the reality of such a life and of the possibility of attaining it is firmly fixed in the mind. Such conviction, which consists of a steadfast belief in the supremacy of purity and goodness over desire and passion, is called *faith*. Such faith is the stay, support, and comfort of the man who, while yet in the darkness, is searching earnestly for the Light, which breaks upon him for the first time in all its dazzling splendour and ineffable majesty when he enters the Shining Gateway of Meditation. Without such faith he could not stand for a single day against the trials, failures, and difficulties which beset him continually, much less could he courageously fight and overcome them, and his final conquest and salvation would be impossible.

Upon entering the stage of meditation, faith gradually ripens into knowledge, and the new regenerate life begins to be realised in its quiet wisdom, calm beauty, and ordered strength, and day by day its joy and splendour increase.

The final conquest over sin is now assured. Lust, hatred, anger, covetousness, pride and vanity, desire for pleasure, wealth, and fame, worldly honour and power—all these have become dead things shortly to pass away for ever; there is no more life nor happiness in them; they have no part in the life of the regenerate one, who knows that he can never again go back to them, for now the "old man" of self and sin is dead, and the "new man" of Love and Purity is born within him. He has become (or becomes, as the process of meditation ripens and bears fruit) a new being, one in whom Purity, Love, Wisdom, and Peacefulness are the ruling qualities, and wherein strifes, envies, suspicions, hatreds, and jealousies cannot find lodgment. "Old things have passed away, and, behold, all things have become new"; men and things are seen in a different light, and a new universe is unveiled; there is no confusion; as out of the inner chaos of conflicting desires, passions, and sufferings the new being arises, there arises in the outer world of apparently irreconcilable conditions a new Cosmos, ordered, sequential, harmonious, ineffably glorious, faultless in equity.

Meditation is a process both of *purification* and *adjustment*. Aspiration is the purifying element, and the harmonising power resides in the intellectual train of thought involved.

When the stage of meditation is reached and entered upon, two distinct processes of spiritual transmutation are reached and entered upon, two distinct processes of spiritual transmutation begin to take place, namely:

1. Transmutation of passion
2. Transmutation of affliction

The two conditions proceed simultaneously, as they are interdependent, and act and react one upon the other. Passion and affliction, or sin and suffering, are two aspects of one thing, namely, the *self* in man, that self which is the source of all the troubles which afflict mankind. They represent *power*, but power wrongly used. Passion is a lower manifestation of a divine energy which possesses a higher use and application. Affliction is the limitation and negation of that energy, and is therefore a means of restoring harmony. It says, in effect, to the self-bound man, "Thus far shalt thou go and no farther." The man of meditation transfers the passional energy from the realm of evil (self-following) to the realm of good (self-overcoming). Today he reflects, tomorrow he overcomes his passions, and the third day he rejoices. The mind is drawn from its downward tendency, and is directed upwards. The base metal of error is transmuted into the pure gold of Truth. Lust, hatred, and selfishness disappear; and purity, love, and goodwill take their place. As the stage proceeds, the mind becomes more and more firmly fixed in the higher manifestations, and it becomes increasingly difficult for it to think and act in the lower; and just in the measure that the mind is freed from the lower, violent, and inharmonious activities, just so much is passion transmuted into power, and affliction into bliss.

This means that there is no such thing as affliction to the sinless man. When sin is put away, affliction disappears.

Selfhood is the source of suffering; Truth is the source of bliss.

When the unregenerate man is abused, slandered, misunderstood, or persecuted, it causes him intense suffering; but when these things are brought to bear on the regenerate man, there arises in him the rapture of heavenly bliss. None but he who has put away the great enemy, self, under his feet can fully enter into and understand the saying:

> ye, when men shall revile you, and persecute you, and shall say all manner of evil against you falsely, for my sake. Rejoice, and be exceeding glad.

And why does the righteous (regenerate) man rejoice under those conditions which cause such misery to the unrighteous (unregenerate) man? It is because, having overcome the evil in himself, he ceases to see evil without. To the good man all things are good, and he utilises everything for the good of the world. To him persecution is not an evil; it is a good. Having acquired insight, knowledge, and power, he, by meeting that persecution in a loving spirit, helps and uplifts his persecutors, and accelerates their spiritual progress, though they themselves know it not at the time. Thus he is filled with unspeakable bliss because he has conquered the forces of evil; because, instead of succumbing to those forces, he has learned how to use and direct them for the good and gain of mankind. He is blessed because he is at one with all men, because he is reconciled to the universe, and has brought himself into harmony with the Cosmic Order.

The following symbol will perhaps help the mind of the reader to more readily grasp what has been explained:

LOVE, LIGHT, AND LIFE

KNOWLEDGE

ASPIRATION

PASSION   AFFLICTION

DESIRE

IGNORANCE

LUST. DARKNESS. AND DEATH

There is at first the underworld of *lust, darkness*, and *death*, which is associated with *ignorance*; rooted in this is the foot of the cross—*desire*; in the body of the cross, desire branches out into two arms—the right (active or positive) arm, *passion*, being equalised and balanced by the left (passive or negative) arm of *affliction*; uniting these, and rising out of them at the head of the cross, is *aspiration*; here, wounded and bleeding, rests the thorn-crowned head of humanity; at the end of this, and right at the summit of the cross, is *knowledge*, which, while being at the apex of the self-life, is the base of the Truth-life; and above rises the heavenly world of *Love, Light*, and *Life*.

In this supremely beautiful world the regenerate man lives, even while living on this earth. He has reached Nirvana, the Kingdom of Heaven. He has taken up his cross, and there is no more sin and suffering; desire and passion and affliction are passed away. Harmony is restored, and all is bliss and peace.

The cross is the symbol of pain. Desire is painful, passion is painful, affliction is painful, and aspiration is painful; this is why these things are symbolised by a cross which has two pairs of conflicting poles. Affliction is the harmonising and purifying element in passion; aspiration is the harmonising and purifying element in desire. Where the one is, the other must be also. Take away the one, and the other disappears. Suffering, or affliction, is necessary to counteract passion; aspiration, or prayer, is necessary to purge away desire; but for the regenerate man all these things are ended; he has risen into a new life and a new order of things—the consciousness of purity; lacking nothing, and being at one with all things, he does not need to pray for anything; redeemed and reconciled, contented and in peace, he finds nothing in the universe to hate or fear, and his is both the duty and the power to work without ceasing for the present good and the ultimate salvation of mankind.

Temptation

I know that sorrow follows passion; know
That grief and emptiness and heartache wait
Upon all earthly joys; so am I sad;
Yet Truth must be, and being, can be found;
And though I am in sorrow, this I know–
I shall be glad when I have found the Truth.

The only external tempters of man are the *objects of sensation*. These, however, are powerless *in themselves* until they are reflected in his mind as desirable objects to possess. His only enemy, therefore, is his *coveting of the objects of sensation*. By ceasing to covet objects of sensation, temptation and the painful fighting against impure desires pass away. This ceasing to covet objects of sensation is called the *relinquishing of* desire; it is *the renunciation of the inner defilement*, by which a man ceases to be the slave of outward things, and becomes their master.

Temptation is a growth, a process more or less slow, the duration of which can be measured by the sage who has gained accurate knowledge of the nature of his thoughts and acts and the laws governing them, by virtue of having subjected himself to a long course of training in mental discipline and self-control. It has its five stages, which can be clearly defined, and their development traced with precision. But the man who is still immersed in temptation has, as yet, little or no knowledge of the nature of his thoughts and acts and the laws governing them. He has lived so long in outward things—in the objects of sensation—and has given so little time to introspection and the cleansing of his heart, that he lives in almost total ignorance of the real nature of his thoughts and acts which he thinks and commits every day. To him, temptation seems to be instantaneous, and his powerlessness to combat the sudden and, apparently, unaccountable onslaught, causes him to regard it as a *mystery*, and mystery being the mother of superstition, he may—and usually does—fall back upon some speculative belief to account for his trouble, such as the belief in an invisible Evil Being, or power, outside himself, who suddenly, and without warning, attacks and torments him. Such a superstition renders him more powerless still, for he has sufficient knowledge to understand that he cannot hope to successfully cope with a being more powerful than himself, and of whose whereabouts and tactics he is altogether unacquainted; and so he introduces other beliefs and superstitions which his dilemma seems to necessitate, until at last, in addition to all his sins and sufferings, he becomes burdened with a mass of supernatural beliefs which engross his attention, and take him farther and farther away from the real cause of his difficulty. Meantime he continues to be tempted and to fall, and must do so until by self-subjugation and self-purification he has acquired the ability to trace the relation between cause and effect in his spiritual nature, when, with purified and enlightened vision, he will see that *the moment of temptation is but the fulfilment of those impure desires which he secretly harbours in his own heart.* And, later, with a still purer heart, and when he has gained sufficient control over his wandering thoughts to be able to analyse and understand them, he will see that *the actual moment of temptation itself* has its inception, its growth, and its fruition.

What, then, are the stages in temptation? And how is the process of temptation born in the mind? How does it grow and bear its bitter fruit? The stages are five, and are as follows: 1. *Perception*; 2. *Cogitation*; 3. *Conception*; 4. *Attraction*; and 5. *Desire*.

The first stage is that in which objects of sensation are *perceived as objects*. This is pure perception, and is without sin or defilement. The second stage is that in which objects of sensation are *considered as objects of personal pleasure*. This is a brooding of the mind upon objects, with an undefined groping for pleasurable sensation, and is the beginning of defilement and sin. In the third stage objects of sensation are *conceived as objects of pleasure*. In this stage the objects are associated with certain pleasurable sensations, and these sensations are conceived and called up vividly in the mind. In the fourth stage objects of sensation are *perceived as objects of pleasure*. At this stage the pleasure as connected with the object is distinctly defined, yet there is a confusion of *pleasure* and *object*, so that the two appear as one, and a wish to possess the object arises in the mind; there is also a going out of the mind towards the object. The fifth and last stage is an intense desire, a coveting and lusting to possess the object in order to experience the pleasure and gratification which it will afford. With every repetition, in the mind, of the first four stages, this desire is added to, as fuel is added to fire, and it increases in intensity and ardour until at last the whole being is aflame with a burning passion which is blind to everything but its own immediate pleasure and gratification. And when this painful fruition of thought is reached, a man is said to be tempted. There is a still further stage of Action, which is merely the doing of the thing desired, the outworking of the sin already committed in the mind. From desire to action is but a short step.

The following table will better enable the mind of the reader to grasp the process and principle involved:

INACTION—*HOLINESS; REST*

1. Perception	Objects of Sensation *perceived* as such.
2. Cogitation	Objects of Sensation *considered* as a source of pleasure.
3. Conception	Objects of Sensation *conceived* as affording pleasure.
4. Attraction	Objects of Sensation *perceived* as pleasurable in possession.
5. Desire	Objects of Sensation *coveted* as such: *i.e.*, desired for personal delight and pleasure.

ACTION—*SIN; UNREST*

Every time a man is tempted, he passes, from *Inaction*, through all the five stages in succession, and his fall is a passing on into *Action*. The process varies greatly in duration according to the nature of the temptation and the character of the tempted; but after much yielding and many falls, the mind becomes so familiar with the transition that it passes through all the stages with such rapidity as to make the temptation appear as an instantaneous, indivisible experience.

The sage, however, never loses sight of the duration of time occupied in the process of temptation, but watches its growth and transition; and just as the scientist can measure the time occupied in the transition of sensation from the brain to the bodily extremities, or from the extremities to the brain, which, ordinarily, appears not to occupy duration, so the sage measures (though by a different method) the passage from pure perception to inflamed desire in a sudden experience of temptation.

This knowledge of the nature of temptation destroys its power, or rather its *apparent* power, for power exists in holiness only. Ignorance is at the root of all sin, and it fades away when knowledge is admitted into the mind. Just as darkness and the effects of darkness disappear when light is introduced, so sin and its effects are dispersed when knowledge of one's spiritual nature is acquired and embraced.

How, then, does the sage avoid sin and remain in peace? Knowing the nature of sinful acts—how they are the result of temptation; knowing also the nature of temptation—how it is the end and fruition of a particular train of thought, *he cuts off that train of thought at its commencement*, not allowing his mind to go out into the world of sensation, which is the world of pain and sorrow. He stands over his mind, eternally vigilant, and does not allow his thoughts to pass beyond the safe gates of *pure perception*. To him "all things are pure" because his mind is pure. He sees all objects, whether material or mental, *as they are*, and not as the pleasure-seeker sees them—as objects of personal enjoyment; nor as the tempted one sees them—as sources of evil and pain. His normal sphere, however, is that of *Inaction*, which is perfect holiness and rest. This is a position of entire indifference to considerations of pleasure and pain, regarding all things from the standpoint of *right*, and not from that of *enjoyment*. Is, then, the sage, the sinless one, deprived of all enjoyment? Is his life a dead monotony of inaction—inertia? Truly, he is delivered from all those sensory excitements which the world calls "pleasure," but which conceal, as a mask, the drawn features of pain; and, being released from the bondage of cravings and pleasures, he lives without ceasing in the divine, abiding joy which the pleasure-seeker and the wanderer in sin can neither know nor understand;

but *inaction* in this particular means inaction as regards sin; inaction in the lower animal activities which, being cut off, their energy is transferred to the higher intellectual and moral activities, releasing their power, and giving them untrammelled scope and freedom.

Thus the sage avoids sin by extracting its root within himself, not allowing it to grow into attraction, to blossom into desire, and to bear the bitter fruits of sinful actions. The unwise man, however, allows the thought of pleasure to take root in his mind, where its growth evokes sensations which are pleasant to him, and on these sensations he dwells with enjoyment, thinking in his heart, "So long as I do not commit the sinful act, I am free from sin." He does not know that his thoughts are causes the effects of which are actions, and that there is *no escape from sinful acts for him who dwells in sinful thoughts.* And so the process develops in his mind and blossoms into desire, and in the final moment of temptation (which is but the moment of opportunity brought into prominence by that desire), with the coveted object at his unreserved command, the fall of the man into sinful action is swift and certain.

Regeneration

Submit to naught but nobleness; rejoice
Like a strong athlete straining for the prize,
When thy full strength is tried; be not the slave
Of lusts and cravings and indulgences,
Of disappointments, miseries, and griefs,
Fears, doubts, and lamentations, but control
Thyself with calmness; master that in thee
Which masters others, and which heretofore
Has mastered thee; let not thy passions rule,
But rule thy passions; subjugate thyself
Till passion is transmuted into peace,
And wisdom crown thee; so shalt thou attain
And, by attaining, know.

Having considered and examined the nature of temptation in its five interdependent stages, let us now turn to the process of regeneration, and also consider its nature, so that the reader who has already received some measure of enlightenment may be still further guided in his strenuous climbing towards the Perfect Life.

The five stages in regeneration (already enumerated) are: 1. Reflection; 2. Introspection; 3. Self-analysis; 4. Meditation; and 5. Pure Perception.

The first stage in a pure and true life is that of *thoughtfulness*. The thoughtless cannot enter the right way in life. Only the reflective mind can acquire wisdom. When a man, ceasing to go after enjoyment, brings himself to a standstill in order to examine his position, and to reflect upon the condition of the world and the meaning of life, then he has entered upon the first stage of regeneration. When a man begins to think seriously, and with a deep and noble purpose in view, he has stepped out of the broad way where the thoughtless and the frivolous clutch at the bubbles of pleasure, and has entered the narrow way where the thoughtful and the wise comprehend eternal verities. Such a man's liberation from sin and suffering is already assured; for though he is, as yet, surrounded by much uncertainty, he is already realising a foretaste of the peace which awaits him; his passions, though still strong, are quieter; his mind is calmer and clearer; his intercourse with others is purer and graver; and in his moments of deepest thought he sees, as in a vision, the strength and calmness and wisdom which he knows will one day be his well-earned possessions.

Thus he passes on to the second stage.

Reflecting day by day, with ever-increasing earnestness, upon life in all its phases, he comes to perceive the passions and desires in which men are involved, and realises the sorrows which are connected with their strangely ephemeral existence. He sees the burning fevers of lusts and ambitions and cravings for pleasure, and the chilling agues of anxieties and fears, and the uncertainty of slowly approaching death, and he aspires to know the meaning of it all; is eager to find the source and cause of what seems so sorrowful and inexplicable. Recognising himself as a unit in humanity, as one involved in like passions and sorrows with all other men, he vaguely understands that somehow the secret of all life is inevitably bound up with his own existence, and so, unsatisfied with the surface theories which are based on observation only, and which still leave him subject to passions and sorrows, and the prey of anxieties and fears, he turns his thoughts inwardly upon his own mind, thinking, perchance, that the wished-for revelation of wisdom and peace awaits him there. Thus he becomes *introspective*, and so he passes on to the third stage.

When the introspective habit is fully ripened and acquired, there is called up in the mind a subtle process of inductive thought by the aid of which the innermost recesses of the man's nature, and, therefore, of all humanity, begin to unveil themselves, and yield up their secrets to the penetrating insight of the patient searcher who, unravelling now the tangled threads of thought, and tracing out the warp and woof of the web of life as it is woven in the mental processes and by the swift-flying shuttle of thought, begins, for the first time, to somewhat clearly comprehend the inner causes of human deeds, and the meaning and purpose of existence. As this process of thought is proceeded with, the desires and passions are purified away from the mind; the calmness necessary to a right perception of Truth is acquired; and gradually the fixed principles of things are presented to the comprehension, and the eternal laws of life axe coherently grasped by the understanding.

And now, quietly, and almost as imperceptibly as the soft light of dawn stealing upon the sleeping world, the neophyte, with mind purified, calmed, and controlled, passes into the fourth stage, and opens his long-sleeping eyes upon the rising light of Truth. He becomes habitually meditative, and in meditation he finds the master-key which unlocks the Door of Knowledge. It is at this advanced stage in the process of regeneration that the sinner becomes the saint, and the pupil is transformed into the master; for here the process of transmutation, hitherto slow and painful, is greatly accelerated, so that the spiritual forces formerly spent in pleasures, gratifications, passions, and afflictions are now conserved, controlled, and turned into channels of productive and reproductive thought, and so wisdom is born in the mind, and bliss, and peace.

As skill and power are acquired in meditation, the fifth and last stage is reached, where the perfect insight of the seer and the sage is evolved, so that the facts of life are grasped, and the laws and principles of things stand revealed. Here the man is altogether regenerated, is purified and perfected; all human passions are conquered, and human sorrows transcended. Here things are seen *as they are*; all the intricacies of life stand out naked in the light of Truth, and there is no more doubt and perplexity, no more sin and anguish; for he whose pure and enlightened eyes perceive the hidden causes and effects which operate infallibly in human life—he who knows how the bitter fruits of passion ripen, and where the dark waters of sorrow spring—he it is who no more sins and no more sorrows. Lo! he has come to peace.

The five stages so passed through may be thus presented:

IGNORANCE—*SIN; SUFFERING*

1. Reflection	Deep and earnest thought on the nature and meaning of life.
2. Introspection	Looking inwardly for the causes and effects which operate in life.
3. Self-analysis	Searching the springs of thought and purifying the motives in order to find the truth of life.
4. Meditation	Pure and discriminative thought on the facts and principles of life.
5. Pure Perception	Insight. Direct knowledge of the laws of life.

ENLIGHTENMENT—*PURITY; PEACE*

The whole process of regeneration may be likened to the growth of a plant. At first the small seed of *reflection* is cast into the dark soil of ignorance; then the little rootlets come forth and grope about for light and sustenance (introspection); next the strenuous *self-examination* is as the plant reaching upwards toward the light; and then the development of the bud and opening flower of *meditation*, ending at last in that pure and wise insight which is the spiritual glory of the sage, the perfect flower of enlightenment.

Thus beginning in sin and suffering, and passing through thoughtfulness, self-searching, self-purification, meditation, and insight, the seeker after the pure life and the divine wisdom reaches at last the undefiled habitation of a spotless life, and so passes beyond the dark halls of suffering, knowing the perfect Law.

Actions
and Motives

Obey the Right,
And wrong shall ne'er again assail thy peace,
Nor error hurt thee more: attune thy heart
To Purity, and thou shalt reach the Place
Where sorrow is not, and all evil ends.

It has been said that "the way to hell is paved with good intentions," and one frequently hears sin excused on the ground that it was done with a "good motive."

There are actions which are bad-in-themselves, and there are actions which are good-in-themselves, and good intentions cannot make the former good—selfish intentions cannot make the latter bad. Foremost among actions which are bad-in-themselves are those which are classified as "criminal" by all civilised communities. Thus murder, theft, adultery, libel, etc., are always bad, and it is not necessary to inquire into the motive which prompts them. Black and white remain black and white to all eternity, and are not altered by specious argumentations. A lie is eternally a lie, and no number of good intentions can turn it into a truth. If a man tell a lie with a good intention, he has none the less uttered a lie; if a man speak the truth with a selfish intention, he has none the less spoken the truth.

Besides those actions above mentioned, there are others which, while not classified by the law of the land as criminal, are yet recognised as wrong by nearly all intelligent people—actions pertaining to social and family life, and to our everyday relations with our fellowmen. Thus when a child wilfully violates its duty to its parents, the father does not stop to inquire into the motives of the child, but metes out the due correction, because the act of disobedience is *wrong-in-itself.*

The reader may here ask, "In being taught, then, to regard the motive, the condition of heart, as all important, and the act as secondary, have we been taught wrongly?" No, you have not. The motive *is* all important, for it determines the nature of the act, and here we must distinguish between *intentions* and *motives*. When people speak of good and bad motives, they nearly always mean good or bad intentions—that is, the action is done with a certain object, good or bad, in view. The motive is the deeply seated *cause* in the mind, the habitual condition of heart; the intention is the *purpose* in view. Thus an act may spring from an impure motive, yet be done with the best intention. It is possible for one to be involved in wrong motives, and yet at the same time to be so charged with good intentions as to be continually intruding himself on other people, and interfering in their business and their lives under the delusion that they "need his help."

Intentions are more or less superficial, and are largely matters of impulse, while motives are more deeply seated, and are concerned with a man's fixed moral condition. A man may do an action today with a good intention, and in a few weeks time do the same action with a bad intention; but in both instances the motive underlying the action will be the same.

In reality a wrong act cannot spring from a right motive, although it may be guided by a good intention. A man who can resort, whether habitually or under stress of temptation, to murder, theft, lying, or other actions known as bad, is in a dark, confused condition of mind, and is not capable of acting from right motives. Such acts can only spring from an impure source; and this is why the

Great Teachers rarely refer to motives, but always refer to actions. In their precepts they tell us what actions are bad and what are good, without any reference to motive, for the bad and good acts-in-themselves are the fruits of bad and good motives. "By their fruits you shall know them."

In being exhorted to "judge not," we are not taught to persuade ourselves that grapes are figs and figs grapes, but must employ our judgment in clearly distinguishing between the two; so in like manner must we distinguish with unmistakable clearness between bad actions and good actions, so as to avoid the former and embrace the latter; for only in this way can one purify his heart and render himself capable of acting from right motives. A clear perception of what is bad or good, both in ourselves and others, is not false judgment, it is wisdom. It is only when one harbours groundless suspicion about others, and reads into their actions bad and selfish intentions, that he falls into that judging against which we are warned, and which is so pernicious.

There is no need to doubt the good intentions of those about us, while, at the same time, being fully alive to a knowledge of those bad actions which were better left undone, and those good actions which were better done; taking care not to do the former, and to do the latter ourselves, thus teaching by our lives instead of accusing and condemning others. Numberless wrong actions are committed every day with good intentions; and this is why so many good purposes are frustrated and end in disappointment, because the underlying motive is impure, and the good fruit which is sought does not appear; the act is out of harmony with the good intent; the means are not adapted to the end. Bad actions bring forth bitter fruit; good actions bring forth sweet fruit.

The law runs, "Thou shalt not kill; thou shalt not steal; thou shalt not commit adultery"; not "Thou shalt not kill, steal, or commit adultery *with a bad motive.*"

Wrong actions are always accompanied with self-delusion, and the chief form which such self-delusion assumes is that of self-justification. If a man flatter himself that he can commit a sinful act, and yet be free from sin because he is prompted by a "pure motive," no limit can be set to the evil which he may commit.

It will be found that bad actions, in the majority of instances, are accompanied with good intentions. The object of the slanderer generally is to protect his fellow-men from one another. Troubled with foolish suspicions, or smarting under the thought of injury, he warns men against each other, speaking only of their bad qualities, and, in his eagerness, distorting the truth. His intention is good, namely, to protect his neighbours; but his motive is bad, namely, hatred of those whom he slanders. Such a man's good intention is frustrated by his bad action, and he at last only succeeds in separating himself from all truth-loving people.

The sore of a bad action is not cured by plastering it over with good intentions, nor is the cause of the defilement removed from the heart.

Men who are involved in bad actions cannot work from pure motives. An issue of foul water always proceeds from an impure source; and an issue of impure actions proceeds from a heart that is defiled.

It greatly simplifies life, and solves all complex problems of conduct, when certain actions are recognised as eternally bad, and others as eternally good, and the bad are for ever abandoned, and final refuge is taken in the good.

The wise and good perform good actions; and motive, act, and intention being harmoniously adjusted, their lives are powerful for good, and free from disappointment, and the good fruit of their efforts appears in due season. They do not need to defend their actions by subtle and specious arguments, not to enter into interminable metaphysical speculations concerning motives; but are content to act, and to leave their actions to bear their own fruit.

Let us not try to persuade ourselves that our good intentions will wipe out the results of our bad actions; but let us resort to the practice of good actions; for only in this way can we acquire goodness; only thus can the life be established on fixed principles, and the mind be rendered capable of comprehending, and working from, pure motives.

Morality and Religion

The wise man
By adding thought to thought and deed to deed
In ways of good, buildeth his character.
Little by little he accomplishes
His noble ends; in quiet patience works
   Diligently.
       Daily he builds into his heart and mind
Pure thoughts, high aspirations, selfless deeds,
Until at last the edifice of Truth
Is finished, and behold! there rises and appears
The Temple of Perfection.

There is no surer indication of confusion and decadence in spiritual matters than the severance of morality from religion. "He is a highly moral man, but he is not religious"; "He is exceptionally good and virtuous, but is not at all spiritual," are common expressions on the lips of large numbers of people who thus regard religion as something quite distinct from goodness, purity, and right-living.

If religion be regarded merely and only as worship combined with adherence to a particular form of faith, then it would be correct to say, "He is a very good man, but is not religious," in some instances, just as it would be equally correct to say, "He is an immoral man, but is very religious," in other instances, for murderers, thieves, and other evil-doers are sometimes devout worshippers and zealous adherents to a creed.

Such a narrowing down of religion, however, would render much of the Sermon on the Mount superfluous, from a religious point of view, and would lead to the confounding of the *means* of religion with its *end*, the idolising of the *letter* of religion to the exclusion of the *spirit*; and this is what actually occurs when morality is severed from religion, and is regarded as something alien and distinct from it.

Religion, however, has a broader significance than this, and the most obscure creed embodies in its ritual some longing human cry for that goodness, that virtue, that morality, which many, with thoughtless judgment, divorce from religion. And is not a life of moral excellence, of good and noble character, of pure-heartedness, the very end and object of religion? Is it not the substance and spirit, of which worship and adherence to a form of faith are but the shadow and letter?

In religion, as in other things, there are the means and the end, the methods and the attainment. Worship, beliefs about God, adherence to creeds—these are some of the means; goodness, virtue, morality—these are the end. The methods are many and various, and they are embodied in countless forms of faith; but the end is one—it is moral grandeur!

Thus the moral man, far from being irreligous because he may not openly profess some form of worship, possesses the substance of religion, diffuses its spirit, has attained its end; and when the sweet kernel of religion is found and enjoyed, the shell, protective and necessary in its place, has served its purpose, and may be dispensed with.

Let not this, however, be misunderstood. The "moral" man does not refer to one who has only the outward form of morality, appearing moral in the eyes of the world, but keeping his vices secret; nor does it refer to him whose morality extends only to legal limits; nor to those who are proud of their morality—for pride is the reverse of moral—but to those who delight in purity, who are gracious, gentle, unselfish, and thoughtful, who, being good at heart, pour forth the fragrance of pure thoughts and good deeds. By the "moral" is meant the good, the pure, the noble, and the true-hearted.

A man may call himself Christian, Jew, Buddhist, Mohammedan, Hindu—or by any other name—and be immoral; but if one is pure-hearted, if he is true and noble and beautiful in character—in a word, if he is moral—then he is an inhabitant of the "Holy City" in which there is "no temple"; he is, by example and influence, a regenerator of mankind; he is one of the company of the Children of Light.

Memory,
Repetition,
and Habit

I shall gain,
By purity and strong self-mastery,
The awakened vision that doth set men free
From painful slumber and the night of grief.

When a particular combination of words has been repeated a number of times, it is said to have been committed to memory—that is, it can then be repeated without visual reference to the words themselves, and without pause or effort; indeed, the words have then a tendency to repeat themselves in the mind, and sometimes people are troubled with the ringing of a refrain, or the repetition of a sentence in the mind, which they find it very difficult to get rid of and forget.

There is a sense in which the whole of life is a process of committing to memory. At first there is *act*, from act springs *experience*, from experience arises *recollection*, from recollection *repetition*, and from repetition is formed *habit*; hence proceeds impulse, faculty, character, individualised existence.

Life is a repetition of the same things over again. There is very little difference between the days and years in the life of a man; one is almost entirely a repetition of the other. Every being is an accumulation of experiences gathered, learnt, and woven into the life by a ceaseless series of repetitions extending over an incalculable number of lives which thread their way through eons of time.

The life of a man, from the germ-cell to maturity, is a repetition, in synthesis, of the entire process of evolution. There is a cosmic memory at the root of all growth and progress, which is an informing and sustaining principle in the process of evolution.

The sensuous memory of man is fickle and ephemeral, but the supersensuous memory which is inherent in all matter, building up forms and faculty, is infallible in its reproduction of experiences.

Life is ceaseless reiteration. Nature ever travels over old and familiar ground. Man is daily repeating that which he has learnt, though the schools of experience in which the lessons were acquired may be long forgotten; but the acquired habit is not forgotten; it is carried forward and continues to act. The unconscious and automatic ease which marks the play of faculty is not the ready-made mechanism of an arbitrary creator; it is *skill acquired by practice*; it is the consummation of millions of repetitions of the same thought and act.

Thoughts and deeds long persisted in become at last spontaneous impulses.

It is a profound truth that "there is nothing new under the sun." It is possible and highly probable that, in the round of eternity, even all our modern inventions and mechanical marvels have been produced innumerable times on this or other worlds. In this world, new combinations of matter appear from time to time, but are they new in the universe? Who dare say that, in the mind which overarches eternity, the cosmic memory is not reproducing things long since fashioned out of itself?

Nothing can be added to, or taken from, the universe. Its matter can neither be increased nor decreased. Chemical combinations of matter vary, but matter itself cannot vary. Life likewise does not change. In the forms of life there is continuous flux, but in the principle of life there is no increase or diminution. Forms come forth only to retreat and disappear; but that which disappears is not lost; the memory of it is retained, and it continues to be repeated. Eternal disintegration is balanced by eternal restitution.

The mind of man is not separate from the Eternal Mind; in its daily repetitions is indelibly written the record of all its past. *Character is an accumulation of deeds.* Each man is the last reckoning in the long sum of evolution, and there is no falsification of the account. The mind continues to automatically perform the habit which encloses a million repetitions of the same deed. Compared with this ineffaceable, unconscious memory, the memory of three score years and ten is as a fading vapour to an Egyptian Pyramid. The tendencies, impulses, and habits of which a man is a victim are the repetitions of his accumulated deeds. They enfold the destiny which he has wrought. The grace, goodness, and genius which a man exhibits without conscious effort are the fruits of the accumulated labours of his mind. He repeats with ease that which was learned by painful labour. The wise man sees a reflection of himself in the fate which overtakes him.

Life flows in channels. Every man is in a rut. Men tell their fellows to "get out of their ruts," but they themselves are in ruts of another kind. The flow of law, of nature, cannot be avoided, but it can be utilised. We cannot avoid ruts, but we can avoid bad ones; we can follow along good ones.

In their training and education, the children of today are strictly Confined to ways which are worn by the feet of a thousand generations. In his fixed habits and characteristics, the man of today is reviving the actions of a thousand lives.

It is true that men are bound; but it is equally true that they can unbind. The law by which a man becomes the sorrowful victim of his own wrong deeds is a blessed, and not a cursed, law; for by the same law he can become the instrument of all that is good. Habits chain a man, but he himself forged the links. He whose inner eye has opened to perceive the law does not complain. The bondage of evil is a heavy slavery, but the bondage of good is a blessed service.

The will of man is powerless to alter the law of life, but it is powerful to obey it. The Great Law makes for good; it puts a heavy penalty on evil. Man can break his chains, and shake himself free; and when he enters earnestly upon the work of self-liberation, all the universe will be with him in his labour. Repetition and habit he cannot avoid, but he can set going repetitions that are harmonious; he can form habits that will crystallise into pure and noble characteristics.

In the self-built archives of the mind are stored away the entire records of man's evolution. Man is an epitomised history of the world. In his outbursts of rage we hear again the roar of the lion in the forest; in his selfish schemings to secure his coveted ends we see the tiger stalking its prey; his lusts, revenges, hatreds, and fears are the instinct born of primeval experiences. The universe does not forget; life remembers and restores.

Between the sensuous and the supersensuous worlds is the Lethean stream, the river of forgetfulness. Only he who has passed into the supersensuous world—the world of pure goodness—remembers with the Memory of Life which transcends a million deaths. Only he whose will obeys the Universal Will, whose heart is in harmony with the Cosmic Order, receives the vision which pierces through the vale of time and matter, and sees the before and the beyond.

Man quickly forgets, and it is well that he forgets; the universe remembers and records. The repetition of an evil deed is its own retribution; the repetition of a good deed is its own reward. The deepest punishment of evil is evil; the highest reward of good is good. When a deed is done, it is not ended; it is but begun; it remains with the doer—to curse him, if evil; to bless him, if good. Deeds accumulate by repetition, and they remain as character, and in character is both curse and blessing.

Suffering inheres in the discordant repetition of evil; bliss inheres in the rhythmic repetitions of good. Seeing that we cannot escape the law of repetition, let us choose to do those things which are good; and as one establishes habits of purity, the divine memory will be awakened within him.

Words
and Wisdom

I would find
Where Wisdom is, where Peace abides, where Truth,
Majestic, changeless, and eternal, stands
Untouched by the illusions of the world;
For surely there is Knowledge, Truth, and Peace
For him who seeks.

Thoughts, words, acts—these combine to make up the entire life of every individual. Words and acts are thoughts expressed. We think in words. In the process of thinking, words are stored up in the consciousness, where they await expression and use as occasion may call them forth.

Words fit the mind which received them; they are the tally of the intellect which uses them. The meaner the mind, the more meagre is the vocabulary. A limited and a capacious intellect alike expresses itself through a limited and an extensive use of words. A great mind expresses itself by the vehicle of flowing and noble language.

Words stand for conceptions. Conceptions are embodied in words. At the moment that a conception is formed in the mind, its corresponding word arises in the thought. Conceptions and words cannot be hidden away indefinitely. Sooner or later they will come forth into the outer world of expression. The matter of the universe is in ceaseless circulation. Its hidden things are continuously coming forth into open and visible life. Likewise the mental operations of men are ever in active circulation, and their hidden thoughts are daily expressing themselves in words and acts. The words and actions of every man are determined by the thoughts in which he habitually dwells.

Speech is audible thought. A man reveals himself through his speech. Whether he is pure or impure, foolish or wise, he makes his inner condition known through his speech. The foolish man is known by the way in which he talks; the wise man is known by the purity, gravity, and excellence of his speech. "He who would gain a knowledge of men," says Confucius, "must first learn to understand the meaning of words."

All wise men, saints, and great teachers have declared that the first step in wisdom is to control the tongue. The disciple of speech is a mental disciple. When a man controls his tongue, he controls his mind; when he purifies his speech, he purifies his mind. Speech and mind cannot be separated. They are two aspects of character.

A man may read Scripture, study religions, and practise mystical arts; but if he allows his tongue to run loosely, he will be as foolish at the end of all his labours as he was at the beginning.

A man may not read Scripture, nor study religions, nor practise ascetic arts; but if he controls his tongue, and studies how to speak wisely and well, he will become wise.

Wisdom is perceived in the words which are its expression. We speak of certain men—of Shakespeare for instance—as being wise. We never saw Shakespeare, and we know very little of his life; how, then, do we know he was wise? By his words only. Where there are wise words, we know there is a wise mind. A foolish man may, like a parrot, *repeat* wise words, but a wise man *frames* wise sentences; his wisdom is shown in originally expressed language.

Why do men speak of words as being bad or good, degrading or inspiring, low or lofty, weak or strong? Is it not because they unconsciously recognise that words cannot be dissociated from thoughts? Why do pure-minded people avoid a man who habitually uses impure language? Is it not because they know that such words proceed from an unclean mind?

It is impossible for any being to give utterance to words which are not already lodged in his mind in the form of thought. The impure mind cannot speak pure words; the pure mind cannot speak impure words. The ignorant cannot speak learnedly, nor the learned ignorantly. The foolish man cannot speak wisely, nor the wise foolishly.

Altered speech follows an altered mind. When a man turns from evil to good, his conversation becomes cleansed. As a man increases in wisdom, he watches, modifies, and perfects his speech.

If the foolish and the wise are known by their words, what, then, is the speech of folly, and what the language of wisdom?

A man is foolish:

If he talks aimlessly and incoherently.
If he engages in impure conversations
If he utters falsehood.
If he speaks ill of the absent, and carries about
    evil reports concerning others.
If he frames flattering words.
If he utters violent and abusive words.
If his speech is irreverent, and his words are
    directed against the great and good.
If he speaks in praise of himself.

A man is wise:

If he talks with purpose and intelligence.
If his conversation is chaste.
If he utters words of sincerity and truth.
If he speaks well of, and in defence of, the absent.
If he speaks words of virtuous reproof.
If his speech is gentle and kindly.
If he talks reverently of the great and good.
If he speaks in praise of others.

We are all, now and always, justified and condemned by our words. The law of Truth is not held in abeyance, and every day is judgment day. For "every idle word" which one speaks he is at once "called to account" in an immediate and certain loss of happiness and influence. By the words which we habitually utter we publish to the universe the degree of our intelligence and the standard of our morality, and receive back through them the judgment of the world. The fool thinks he is harshly judged and badly treated by others, not knowing that his real scourge is his own ungoverned tongue.

To control the tongue, to discipline the speech, to strive for the use of purer and gentler words—this is a very lowly thing, and one that is much despised; but it cannot be neglected by him who eagerly aspires to walk the way of wisdom.

Truth Made Manifest

Upon the lofty Summits of the Truth,
Where clouds and darkness are not, and
    where rests
Eternal Splendour; there, abiding Joy
Awaits thy coming.
Be watchful, fearless, faithful, patient, pure:
By earnest meditation sound the depths
Profound of life, and scale the heights sublime
Of Love and Wisdom.

Truth is rendered visible through the media of deeds. It is something seen and not heard. Words do not contain the Truth; they only symbolise it. Good deeds are the only vessels which contain Truth.

It has been frequently said that *being* must precede *doing*. Being always does precede doing; but being and doing cannot be arbitrarily separated. A man's deeds are the expression of himself. Acts are the language of Reality. If a man's inner being is allied to Truth, his deeds will speak it forth; if with error, his deeds will make manifest that error.

No man can hide what he is. He must necessarily act, and every time he acts he reveals himself.

In the light of Reality no man can deceive humanity or the universe; but he can deceive himself.

Deeds of purity, love, gentleness, patience, humility, compassion, and wisdom are Truth made manifest. These qualities cannot be contained between the covers of a book, but only the words which refer to them; they are Life.

Deeds of impurity, hatred, anger, pride, vanity, and folly are error making itself known. A man's deeds are the publication of himself to the world.

Truth cannot be comprehended through reading, but only by correcting and converting one's self. Precepts are aids to the acquirement of wisdom, but wisdom is acquired only by practice.

If a man would know what measure of Truth he possesses, he should ask himself, "What am I? What are my deeds?"

Men dispute about words, thinking that Truth is heard and read. Truth is neither heard nor read; it is *seen*.

Good deeds are the visible embodiments of Truth; they are messengers of Knowledge; angels of Wisdom; but the eye of error is dark, and cannot see them.

Spiritual Humility

Who would be the companion of the wise,
And know the Cosmic Splendour; he must stoop
Who seeks to stand; must fall who fain would rise;
Must know the low, ascending to the high;
He who would know the Great must not disdain
To diligently wait upon the small:
He wisdom finds who finds humility.

Throughout the Sacred Scriptures of all religions there runs, like a silver thread, the teaching of Humility. Not only all the Scriptures, but the sages of all time have declared that only through the portal of humility is it possible for man to enter into the possession of the Life of Truth; and as that life is entirely of a Spiritual Nature, so the humility that leads to it is purely and absolutely spiritual; and being such, it can never be materialised, can never be embodied in a dogma, or laid down as a formula. It is not an outward thing, nor does it consist of that practice of self-abasement that has usurped its name.

But priests have taught, and many have been led to believe, that self-depreciation is true humility, while in reality it is its extreme antithesis. Self-depreciation is self-degradation; nay, it is even a sort of self-destruction, it is spiritual suicide. The man who believes that all his righteousness is as filthy rags, that there is no good thing in him, and that he can never rise by any effort of his own, is, by that very attitude of his mind, rendering himself impotent; he is strangling the Spirit; he is undermining and disintegrating all that is highest and noblest in his character. Instead of building up his character he is engaged in despoiling it, "As a man thinketh in his heart, so is he"; what our thoughts are, such are our characters. We are in reality beings composed of thoughts; thoughts are the bricks which we are continually laying down in the building of our souls. If we put a large percentage of rotten bricks into the building, we shall build but a miserable hovel, and every self-depreciating thought is a brick that is already crumbling. It will be found to be a rule marvellously accurate in its application that those who continually live in this attitude of self-depreciation are throughout life, or, at any rate, until they strike a nobler attitude, wretched failures. I can bring to my mind many such men that I have known. How can it be otherwise? How can a man who has no faith in himself ever win the confidence of others, or accomplish anything worthy? Moreover, such a man has not, cannot possibly have, any faith in human nature; despising himself, he despises all; and as a result, by the unerring law of cause and effect, all men despise him. Yet it is a strange fact that the men who maintain this faith-destroying attitude of mind invariably profess to have the greatest faith in God; yea, look upon it as an infallible witness to their superior spiritual faith. But I ask this question, Does not true faith, like true charity, begin at home? In the growth of the soul faith in one's self comes first, next faith in human nature, and finally faith in God. That faith which professes to have the latter to the exclusion of the two former is false faith, the outcome of false humility.

Another kind of false humility is that of *personal abasement* to an individual or to established authority. This is humility materialised or subverted. It is the worship of Dagon, the bowing of the knee to Baal, the slavish adoration of the Golden Calf. No man can persist in it without undermining his character, and ultimately dissipating his spiritual and mental energies. Humility to man or to any temporal authority is degrading and slavish; humility to the Most High is grandly beautiful.

Spiritual humility is closely allied to faith, and the more there is of humility the more there is of faith. It is the key-note of all real greatness. In proof of this I have only to refer to the great sages, saints, and reformers of all time. The greatest of them are those who had the greatest share of spiritual humility. True humility, as distinguished from false, has a strengthening power, an upbuilding force. It inspires and invigorates the soul, spurring it to greater and ever greater endeavour.

Of what, then, does this humility consist? Is it the bending of the knee to ask personal favours of Deity? Is it the blind petitioning of God to accomplish for us our petty and narrow designs? Nay, these are its counterfeits. True humility is far above and beyond all this. It is the deepest and holiest aspiration of the human heart, where deep within, hidden from all sacrilegious gaze, it works, a silent mighty power, purifying, transforming, the man of flesh and self; entering its solitary grandeur, the alienated soul returns to the footstool of its God, and bathes, in blissful rapture, in the light of His all-embracing Love. It is a state that can only be entered into by rising above *one's lower self*. It is in fact the submergence of the self in the *non-self*; the submission of passion and intellect to the Supreme; it is the attitude of a human soul adoring its highest conceptions.

Such humility takes its possessor above all that is mean and poor in his nature, into the very presence of God, making him calm, strong, noble, self-reliant, and Godlike. It is the Wine of Life to all aspiring souls. The soul that has not felt its power is dead.

It may sound like a paradox, but it is nevertheless true, that the more a man has of humility the more he has of *independence*. But the seeming paradox will be made clear if we think for a moment of the lives of such teachers of humility as Jesus, Buddha, Confucius, Socrates, Jacob Boehme, George Fox, and indeed of all the great religious reformers. These men walked erect, because, yielding themselves up to the simplicity of humility, they walked with God.

The humility that causes a man to go, metaphorically speaking, on all fours is spurious, and is as debasing and destructive as the real humility is elevating and strengthening. Why should we go amongst our fellows like cringing, fearful beasts, calling ourselves miserable sinners? Shall we ever rise above sin by so doing? Is it possible to rise by ceaselessly contemplating our absolute unworthiness?

No, we can only rise by continually contemplating the Highest. There may be much that is unworthy in a man's heart, but there is also a sacredness, a dignity, a divinity about it; let us dwell upon that. Let us continually contemplate the goodness, the purity, and the essential beauty of human nature. Let us ceaselessly search for the Divinity in our own souls, and, finding it through the door of humility, we shall then recognise the invisible God in all men. By so doing, we rise above the binding limitations of our selfish desires, and enter the larger, healthier, holier life of Love.

Spiritual Strength

All things are holy to the holy mind,
All uses are legitimate and pure,
All occupations blest and sanctified,
And every day a Sabbath.

A clear and firm head must precede and accompany a clean and gentle heart. Without the first the second is impossible, for the qualities of purity and gentleness can only be reached through a clear perception of right and wrong, and by the exercise of an irresistible will. The strength of a powerful animal, or of that animal force in man which enables him to gain the victory over others by attack and resistance, is weakness compared with that quiet, patient, invincible will by which a man overcomes himself, and tames to obedience, and trains to the service of holy purposes, the savage passions of his nature.

Every dog can bark and fight, and every foolish man can rail, abuse, fence with hard words, and give way to fits of bad temper; these things are easy and natural to him, and require no effort and no strength. But the wise man puts away all such follies, and trains himself in self-control—trains himself to act unerringly from fixed principles, and not from the fleeting impulses of an unstable nature.

He who succeeds in so training himself is able to train others, in a small degree by precept, but largely and chiefly by practice or example, for it is pre-eminently the prerogative of the wise to teach by their actions. The mockeries of Herod, the accusations of the people, and the fanatical persecutions of the priests all failed to draw from Jesus the word of complaint, bitterness, or self-defence. Such sublime acts of silence and self-control continue to reach, for ages, both individuals and nations, with far greater power and effect than all the words and books uttered and written by the world's vast army of priests and learned commentators.

To retaliate and fight belongs to the animal in man as it belongs to the beast of the forest; but to refuse to be swayed from the practice of a divine principle by any external pressure—to stand firm and unalterable in goodness and truth alike amid blame and praise—this belongs to the divine in man and in the universe.

To alter one's conduct in order to please others, or to avoid their censure or misunderstanding can never lead to spiritual strength.

That divine kindness which always accompanies spiritual understanding and strength is something very different from merely saying pleasant words—for pleasant words are not always true words—but consists in doing *what is best for the eternal welfare of the other person or persons.*

The weak father, who is unfit to train children, only considers how he can escape trouble with his children, and so he slurs over their acts of disobedience and selfishness, and tries to please them. But the strong father, who considers the future character and welfare of his children, knows how and when to administer a severe reproof, fully understanding that the few minutes' pain caused by his rebuke may save his child from years of suffering as a result of loose living which is fostered by parental neglect. The strong, kind, unselfish father, whose care is for his children's good, and not for his own immediate comfort, knows not only how to be tender in affection, but tender in discipline, knows how to stretch out the strong and (to the child at the time) severe arm of restraint to save his little ones when they would ignorantly wander away in wrong paths.

So the man of spiritual strength cannot be merely a weak framer of smooth words, but a doer of right actions, an utterer of words that are vital and true, and, therefore, eternally kind.

The spiritually weak man shrinks from right when it is brought (as by its nature it must be brought) in opposition to his desires, and he embraces sin because it is pleasant. The spiritually strong man shrinks from sin, more especially when it is presented to him in a pleasant garb, and embraces right, even though by so doing he will bring upon himself the odium of those who are ignorant of divine principles and their beneficent application.

The man of spiritual understanding is as unbending as a bar of steel where right is concerned, knowing that right alone is good; he is as unresisting as water where self is concerned, knowing that self alone is evil. Acting from imperishable principles and not from the fleeting desires of self, his actions partake of the imperishable nature of the principles from which they spring, and continue to afford instruction and inspiration through unnumbered generations.

It is always the portion of one who so acts to be misunderstood. The majority live in their desires and impulses, following them blindly as they are brought into operation by external stimuli, and do not understand what is meant by acting dispassionately from right and fixed principles, with entire freedom from self-interest. Such will necessarily misunderstand and misjudge the right-doer, regarding him as cold and cruel in his unbending adherence to right, or as weak and cowardly in his quiet refusal to passionately defend himself. He will, therefore, "be accused of many things"; but this will not cause him any suffering, nor will he be troubled or disturbed thereby, for the truth which he practises is a source of perpetual joy, and he will be at rest in the knowledge that there are those who will understand and follow, that he is working for the ultimate good even of his accusers, and that, by manifesting the truth in his daily actions, he is in the company of those divinely strong ones who are leading the world into ways of quietness and peace.

James Allen: A Memoir

By Lily L. Allen

from *The Epoch* (February–March 1912)

> *Unto pure devotion*
> *Devote thyself: with perfect meditation*
> *Comes perfect act, and the right-hearted rise—*
> *More certainly because they seek no gain—*
> *Forth from the bands of body, step by step.*
> *To highest seats of bliss.*

James Allen was born in Leicester, England, on November 28th, 1864. His father, at one time a very prosperous manufacturer, was especially fond of "Jim," and before great financial failures overtook him, he would often look at the delicate, refined boy, poring over his books, and would say, "My boy, I'll make a scholar of you."

The Father was a high type of man intellectually, and a great reader, so could appreciate the evident thirst for education and knowledge which he observed in his quiet studious boy.

As a young child he was very delicate and nervous, often suffering untold agony during his school days through the misunderstanding harshness of some of his school teachers, and others with whom he was forced to associate, though he retained always the tenderest memories of others—one or two of his teachers in particular, who no doubt are still living.

He loved to get alone with his books, and many a time he has drawn a vivid picture for me, of the hours he spent with his precious books in his favourite corner by the home fire; his father, whom he dearly loved, in his arm chair opposite also deeply engrossed in his favourite authors. On such evenings he would question his father on some of the profound thoughts that surged through his soul— thoughts he could scarcely form into words—and the father, unable to answer, would gaze at him long over his spectacles, and at last say: "My boy, my boy, you have lived before"—and when the boy eagerly but reverently would suggest an answer to his own question, the father would grow silent and thoughtful, as though he *sensed* the future man and his mission, as he looked at the boy and listened to his words—and many a time he was heard to remark, "Such knowledge comes not in one short life."

There were times when the boy startled those about him into a deep concern for his health, and they would beg him not to *think so much*, and in after years he often smiled when he recalled how his father would say—"Jim, we will have you in the Churchyard soon, if you think so much."

Not that he was by any means unlike other boys where games were concerned. He could play leap-frog and marbles with the best of them, and those who knew him as a man—those who were privileged to meet him at "Bryngoleu"—will remember how he could enter into a game with all his heart. Badminton he delighted in during the summer evenings, or whenever he felt he could.

About three years after our marriage, when our little Nora was about eighteen months old, and he about thirty-three, I realized a great change coming over him, and knew that he was renouncing everything that most men hold dear that he might find Truth, and lead the weary sin-stricken world to Peace. He at that time commenced the practice of rising early in the morning, at times long before daylight, that he might go out on the hills—like One of old—to commune with God, and meditate on Divine things. I do not claim to have understood him fully in those days. The light in which he lived and moved was far too white for my earth-bound eyes to see, and a *sense of it only* was beginning to dawn upon me. But I knew I dare not stay him or hold him back, though at times my woman's heart cried out to do so, waiting him all my own, and not then understanding his divine mission.

Then came his first book, "From Poverty to Power." This book is considered by many his best book. It has passed into many editions, and tens of thousands have been sold all over the world, both authorized and pirated editions, for perhaps no author's works have been more pirated than those of James Allen.

As a private secretary he worked from 9 a.m. to 6 p.m., and used every moment out of office writing his books. Soon after the publication of "From Poverty to Power" came "All These Things Added," and then "As a Man Thinketh," a book perhaps better known and more widely read than any other from his pen.

About this time, too, the "Light of Reason" was founded and he gave up all his time to the work of editing the Magazine, at the same time carrying on a voluminous correspondence with searchers after Truth all over the world. And ever as the years went by he kept straight on, and never once looked back or swerved from the path of holiness. Oh, it was a blessed thing indeed to be the chosen one to walk by the side of his earthly body, and to watch the glory dawning upon him!

He took a keen interest in many scientific subjects, and always eagerly read the latest discovery in astronomy, and he delighted in geology and botany. Among his favourite books I find Shakespeare, Milton, Emerson, Browning, The Bhagavad-Gita, the Tao-Tea-King of Lao-Tze, the Light of Asia, the Gospel of Buddha, Walt Whitman, Dr. Bucke's Cosmic Consciousness, and the Holy Bible.

He might have written on a wide range of subjects had he chosen to do so, and was often asked for articles on many questions outside his particular work, but he refused to comply, consecrating his whole thought and effort to preach the Gospel of Peace.

When physical suffering overtook him he never once complained, but grandly and patiently bore his pain, hiding it from those around him, and only we who knew and loved him so well, and his kind, tender Doctor, knew how greatly he suffered. And yet he stayed not; still he rose before the dawn to meditate, and commune with God; still he sat at his desk and wrote those words of Light and Life which will ring down through the ages, calling men and women from their sins and sorrows to peace and rest.

Always strong in his complete manhood, though small of stature physically, and as gentle as he was strong, no one ever heard an angry word from those kind lips. Those who served him adored him; those who had business dealings with him trusted and honoured him. Ah! how much my heart prompts me to write of his self-sacrificing life, his tender words, his gentle deeds, his knowledge and his wisdom. But why? Surely there is no need, for do not his books speak in words written by his own hand, and will they not speak to generations yet to come?

About Christmas time I saw the change coming, and understood it not—blind! blind! blind! I could not think it possible that *he* should be taken and *I* left.

But we three—as if we knew—clung closer to each other, and loved one another with a greater love—if that were possible—than ever before. Look at his portrait given with the January "Epoch," and reproduced again in this, and you will see that even then our Beloved, our Teacher and Guide, was letting go his hold on the physical. He was leaving us then, and we didn't know it. Often I had urged him to stop work awhile and rest, but he always gave me the same answer, "My darling, when I stop I must go, don't try to stay my hand."

And so he worked on, until that day, Friday, January 12, 1912, when, about one o'clock he sat down in his chair, and looking at me with a great compassion and yearning in those blessed eyes, he cried out, as he stretched out his arms to me, *"Oh, I have finished, I have finished, I can go no further, I have done."*

Need I say that everything that human aid and human skill could do was done to keep him still with us. Of those last few days I dare scarcely write. How could my pen describe them? And when we knew the end was near, with his dear hands upon my head in blessing, he gave his work and his beloved people into my hands, charging me to bless and help them, until I received the call to give up my stewardship!

"I will help you," he said, "and if I can I shall come to you and be with you often."

Words, blessed words of love and comfort, *for my heart alone* often came from his lips, and a sweet smile ever came over the pale calm face when our little Nora came to kiss him and speak loving words to him, while always the gentle voice breathed the tender words to her—*"My little darling!"*

So calmly, peacefully, quietly, he passed from us at the dawn on Wednesday, January 24, 1912. "Passed from us," did I say? Nay, only the outer garment has passed from our mortal vision. He lives! and when the great grief that tears our hearts at the separation is calmed and stilled, I think that we shall know that he is still with us. We shall again rejoice in his companionship and presence.

When his voice was growing faint and low, I heard him whispering, and leaning down to catch the words I heard—"At last, at last—at home—my wanderings are over"—and then, I heard no more, for my heart was breaking within me, and I felt, for *him* indeed it was "*Home at last!*" but for me—And then, as though he knew my thoughts, he turned and again holding out his hands to me, he said: "I have only one thing more to say to you, my beloved, and that is I love you, and I will be waiting for you; good-bye."

I write this memoir for those who love him, for those who will read it with tender loving hearts, and tearful eyes; for those who will not look critically at the way in which I have tried to tell out of my lonely heart this short story of his life and passing away—for *his* pupils, and, therefore, my friends.

We clothed the mortal remains in *pure white linen*, symbol of his fair, pure life, and so, clasping the photo of the one he loved best upon his bosom—they committed all that remained to the funeral pyre.

About the Author

James Allen was one of the pioneering figures of the self-help movement and modern inspirational thought. A philosophical writer and poet, he is best known for his book *As a Man Thinketh*. Writing about complex subjects such as faith, destiny, love, patience, and religion, he had the unique ability to explain them in a way that is simple and easy to comprehend. He often wrote about cause and effect, as well as overcoming sadness, sorrow and grief.

Allen was born in 1864 in Leicester, England into a working-class family. His father travelled alone to America to find work, but was murdered within days of arriving. With the family now facing economic disaster, Allen, at age 15, was forced to leave school and find work to support them.

During stints as a private secretary and stationer, he found that he could showcase his spiritual and social interests in journalism by writing for the magazine *The Herald of the Golden Age.*

In 1901, when he was 37, Allen published his first book, *From Poverty to Power.* In 1902 he began to publish his own spiritual magazine, *The Light of Reason* (which would be retitled *The Epoch* after his death). Each issue contained announcements, an editorial written by Allen on a different subject each month, and many articles, poems, and quotes written by popular authors of the day and even local, unheard of authors.

His third and most famous book *As a Man Thinketh* was published in 1903. The book's minor popularity enabled him to quit his secretarial work and pursue his writing and editing career full time. He wrote 19 books in all, publishing at least one per year while continuing to publish his magazine, until his death. Allen wrote when he had a message—one that he had lived out in his own life and knew that it was good.

In 1905, Allen organized his magazine subscribers into groups (called "The Brotherhood") that would meet regularly and reported on their meetings each month in the magazine. Allen and his wife, Lily Louisa Oram, whom he had married in 1895, would often travel to these group meetings to give speeches and read articles. Some of Allen's favorite writings, and those he quoted often, include the works of Shakespeare, Milton, Emerson, the Bible, Buddha, Whitman, Trine, and Lao-Tze.

Allen died in 1912 at the age of 47. Following his death, Lily, with the help of their daughter, Nora took over the editing of *The Light of Reason*, now under the name *The Epoch*. Lily continued to publish the magazine until her failing eyesight prevented her from doing so. Lily's life was devoted to spreading the works of her husband until her death at age 84.